THE PICTORAL GUIDE TO TOOTHBRUSH HOLDERS

Marilyn M. Cooper

Price Guide Included

The current values in this book should be used only as a guide. They are not intended to set prices, which vary from one section of the country to another. Auction prices as well as dealer prices vary greatly and are affected by condition as well as demand. Neither the Author nor the Publisher assumes responsibility for any losses that might be incurred as a result of consulting this guide.

Copyright Acknowledgments
(C)W.D.-Walt Disney
(C)W.E.D.-Walt E. Disney
(C)W.D.-Walter Disney
C)FAS-Famous Artist Studio
(C)C.A.-Carl Anderson
(C)F.F.-Fountain Fox
(C)W.D.P.-Walt Disney Productions
(C)K-King
(C)T.L.R.-The Lone Ranger Inc.
(C)G.B.-George Borgfield
(C)M-Muppets

Additional copies of this book may be ordered from:

M.M.C. PUBLISHING
P.O. BOX 55174
HOUSTON, TX. 77255

$19.95 Add $3.00 for postage and handling

Copyright: Marilyn M. Cooper, 1994
Library of Congress Catalog Card Number: 94-96205
ISBN: 0-9642756-0-0

TABLE OF CONTENTS

TOOTH BRUSH HOLDER

This tooth brush holder will delight
the kiddies, it's so gay
They'll want to use it every night
And several times a day!

Author Unknown

ACKNOWLEDGEMENTS

There are so many people I wish to thank for their encouragement in writing this book. My family and friends for their support, understanding, and patience. To my friend, Dorothy Cutler, for introducing me to the joy of collecting and friends made during our years of "treasure hunting" adventures. Al Dobbs Jr. and Nancy Smith, with their exuberance, were the catalysts that really ignited me to write this book.

Most expecially, I thank my dear husband Splawn, for his superb photography and computer skills. Dr. Kay P. Walther for her expert help in editing. The Photo Haus crew, Vi , Lori, Patty, and Marlene for their assistance in the photographic reproductions. The entire staff at IMAGE GRAPHICS with special thanks to Mike Long, Bill Regenberg, and John DeVardo who were so very helpful.

My appreciation to the friends listed below for permitting their toothbrush holders to be photographed and included in the book.

All toothbrush holders are from the Author's Collection except the ones marked by the following symbols:

(B) Mary and Henry Burkhart   (M) Reneé and B.J. Maxcey
(S) Catherine Schulte   (W) Laurie and Jeff Walker

DEDICATION

This book is dedicated to my husband Splawn and our sons and their families. Tres and Cindy Cooper, Alyssa, and Grant. Taylor and Marcia Cooper, Cassie, Riley, and Brady.

And to all Toothbrush Holder Collectors who share the joy and excitement of finding a new piece for their collection.

Happy Collecting!
Marilyn M. Cooper

SHAKER TOPS

1   Baby Bunting -
    Germany, 6 3/4"

2   Little Red Riding Hood -
    Germany, 6 1/4"

3   Old Mother Hubbard -
    Germany, 6 1/4"

4   Peter Rabbit -
    Germany, 6 1/4"

5-10 Reserved

23   Bonzo w/Sidetray, Lustre -
     Germany, 3 5/8", Mouth holds brush

24   Boy Brushing Teeth-Japan, 6 1/2", 2 holes

25   Boy w/Cap and Tie-Japan, 6 1/4", 3 holes

26   Boy w/Dog-Japan, 6", 3 holes
27   Girl w/Dog-Japan, 6", 3 holes

28   Boy on Elephant-Japan, 6 1/4", 3 holes (B)

29   Boy w/Top Hat-Japan, 5 1/2", 2 holes

30   Boy w/Violin-Japan (Goldcastle), 5 1/2", 2 holes

36   Cat-Japan(Goldcastle), 5 3/4", 2 holes

31-35 Reserved

37 Cat, Calico-Japan, 5 1/2", 2 holes

38 Cat w/Bass Fiddle-Japan,
    6", 2 holes

39 Chef-Japan, 5 1/4", 2 holes

40 Children in Auto-Japan
    5", 2 holes

HANGING WITH TRAY OR FEET TO HOLD TOOTHPASTE

41 Children, Big Brother-Japan,
    6 5/8", 3 holes

42 Children, Big Sister-Japan,
    7 1/4", 3 holes

43 Children, Boy w/Basket-Japan, 4 3/4",
    2 holes

44 Children, Girl w/Basket-Japan, 4 1/2",
    2 holes

45 Children, Girl w/Umbrella-Japan, 4
    1/2", 2 holes

46 Children, Boy w/Umbrella-Japan, 4
    3/4", 2 holes

47 Children, Little Sister-Japan, 4 3/4", 2 holes

48 Children, Little Brother-Japan(Goldcastle), 5",
    1 hole

49-54 Reserved

55 Circus Dog-Japan, 4 1/2", 1 hole
56 Circus Elephant-Japan, 5 3/8", 1 hole

57 Clown(large)-Japan, 6", 1 hole
58 Clown(small)-Japan, 4 1/2", 1 hole (B)

59 Clown w/Bug on Nose-Japan, 5 1/8", 3 holes

60 Clown, Juggling-Japan, 5", 3 holes (B)

61   Clown w/Mandolin-Japan,
     6", 1 hole

62   Clown w/Mask-Japan
     (Goldcastle), 5 1/2", Arms
     hold brushes

69   Cow-Japan, 6", 3 holes   (B)

70   Cowboy next to Cactus-Japan,
     5 1/2", 3 holes

63-68 Reserved

71 Dachshund-Japan,
    5 1/4", 2 holes

72 Dog w/Basket-Japan,
    5 3/4", 1 hole

73 Dog, Head Cocked-Japan,
    5 3/4", 1 hole

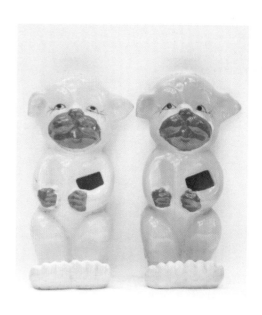

74 Dog, Smiling-Japan,
    5 3/4", 2 holes
74A Same as above, color variant (B)

75 Dog w/Pup & Basket-Japan,
    6 1/4", 3 holes (B)

81 Donkey-Japan(Goldcastle),
    5 3/4", 1 hole

82 Donkey w\Mane-Japan, 5 3/4",
    2 holes, mane holds 1 brush

83 Donald Duck(Bisque)-(C)W.E.D.
    5 1/4", 2 holes

76-80 Reserved

84 Ducky Dandy-Japan, 4 1/4", 2 holes

85 Dutch Girl w/Big Feet-Japan,
    5 3/4", 1 hole

86 Dutch Girl w/Flowers-Japan,
    5 7/8", 1 hole

87 Dutch Boy w/Hands on Hips-
    Japan, 5 1/4", 3 holes   (B)

HANGING WITH TRAY OR FEET TO HOLD TOOTHPASTE

88   Dutch Boy and Girl Kissing-
     Japan, 6 1/4", 2 holes   (B)

93   Dwarfs in Front of Fence (Sleepy and
     Dopey) (Bisque), (C)W.D.-Japan
     3 1/2", 2 holes   (M)

94   Elephant w/Trunk in Air-Japan,
     5 1/2", 3 holes

95   Elephant w/Tusk-Japan,
     5 1/2", 1 hole

89-92 Reserved

96 Genie-Japan(SHOP),
     5 3/4", 3 holes

97 Giraffe-Japan, 6", 3 holes

98 Girl w/Doll-Japan,
     5 3/4", 1 hole (B)
99 Girl w/Dog & Bonnet-Japan,
        5 1/4", 1 hole

100 Girl w/Hat & Dog-Japan (W), 5 1/2",
        1 hole

HANGING WITH TRAY OR FEET TO HOLD TOOTHPASTE

101 Girl Powdering Nose-Japan,
6 1/4", 2 holes

102 Girl w/Basket-Japan,
5 1/4", 2 holes
103 Girl Combing Boy's Hair -
Japan, 5", 2 holes

104 Girl Washing Boy's Face- (C)G.B.,
5", 2 holes

105 Halloween Policeman-Japan,
5", 1 hole

106-110 Reserved

111 Harold Teen-(C)SAS, Japan,
5 1/2", 2 holes (M)

112 Henry & Henrietta(Bisque)-(C)1934CA-
Japan, 4 1/2", 2 holes

113 Horse-Japan, 5", 2 holes

114 Humpty Dumpty(Bisque),
Pat.Pend.-5 1/2", 3 holes

HANGING WITH TRAY OR FEET TO HOLD TOOTHPASTE

115 Indian Chief-Japan,
    4 1/2", 2 holes

116 Kayo-Japan, 5", 2 holes

117 Little Riding Hood -
    Japan, 5 1/2", 2 holes
117A Little Red Riding Hood -
    Japan, 5 1/4", 1 hole

118 Lion-Japan, 6", 2 holes
118A Same as above, color variant (B)

119 Mary Poppins-Japan,
5 3/4", 2 holes

120 Mexican Boy-Japan,
5 1/2", 2 holes

121 Mickey Mouse, Donald Duck,
Minnie Mouse(Bisque)-(C)W.E.D.
Japan(S335), 4 1/2", 2 holes

122 Mickey Mouse & Pluto-(C)W.E.D.,
4 1/2", 2 holes

123 Moon Mullins(C)FAS-Japan,
5 1/4", 2 holes

124 Muggsy(pair)-Japan, 3 1/2", 2 holes
(M)

125 Old King Cole-Japan,
5 1/4", 1 hole

126 Old Woman in Shoe-Japan,
4 1/2", 3 holes

127 Orphan Annie(C)FAS-Japan,
     5 1/4", 1 hole

128 Penguin-Japan, 5 1/2", 3 holes

129 Peter Pumpkin-Eater-Japan,
     4 7/8", 2 holes

130 Peter Rabbit-Japan,
     5 1/2", 2 holes

131 Pirate w/Large Boots-Japan,
5 1/4", 2 holes (B)

132 Pirate w/Sash-Japan,
6", 2 holes

133 Pluto-Japan, 4 5/8", 1 hole

134 Pup, Begging-Japan,
3 7/8", 1 hole
135 Pup, "Brush for Health"-
Japan, 4 1/8", 3 holes

136 Pup, Large Eyes-Japan,
3 1/2", 2 holes

137 Rabbit(Norwood)-Germany,
(T696), 5 1/2", 1 hole

138 Rabbit w/Containers for Brushes-
Japan, 6 1/2", 3 holes

145 Sailors on Anchor-Japan,
5 1/2", 2 holes (B)

146 Scottie Dogs-Japan
       (Goldcastle), 4 1/8", 3 holes

147 "Siesta"-Japan, 6", 1 hole

148 Soldier-Japan, 6 3/4", 1 hole

149 Soldier w/Sash-Japan,
       6", 2 holes

150 The Baker-Japan(Goldcastle),
      5 1/4", 1 hole

151 The Butcher-Japan(Goldcastle),
      5 1/4", 1 hole

152 The Candle Stick Maker-
      Japan(Goldcastle),
      5 1/4", 1 hole

153 The Three Bears-Japan,
      5 ", 2 holes   (B)

154 Tom, Tom, the Piper's Son-
   Japan, 5 3/4", 2 holes

155 Toonerville Trolley(Bisque)-
   (C)FF-Japan, 5 1/2", 2 holes

156 Uncle Walt(C)FAS-Japan,
   5 1/4", 2 holes

157 Uncle Willie(C)FAS-Japan,
   5 1/8", 2 holes

158-165 Reserved

166 Bird-Japan, 4 3/4", 1 hole

167 Bear(Norwood) - Germany,
5 3/4", 1 hole

168 Bear(Chalk)- 6 1/8", 1 hole

169 Bell Hop-Japan(Nagoia),
TRICO, 6 1/2", 2 holes

170 Bonzo w/Tail(7617)-
Japan, 6", 1 hole

171 Bonzo-Japan, 6", 1 hole

172 Carousel (Marked w/Crown),
5", 4 holes

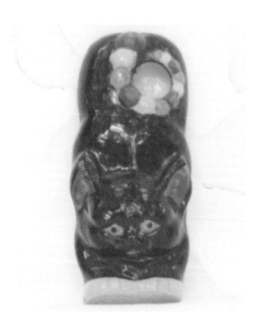

173 Cat, Standing on Front Paws-
Japan, 5 3/8", 1 hole

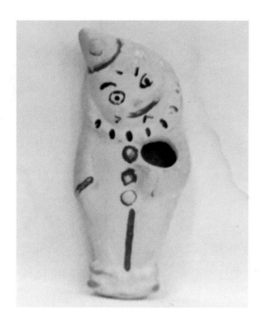

174 Clown(Terra Cotta)-Japan,
5 1/2", 1 hole

175 Clown, Iron 3 3/4",
Arms hold brush   (M)

176 Clown w/Fancy Vest-Japan
(Nagoia), TRICO, Lustre,
6 5/8", 2 holes

177 Clown w/Ruffled Collar -
Japan(Nagoia), TRICO, Lustre,
6 5/8", 2 holes

178 Dog, "The Kirede",
5 1/2", 2 holes

179 Dog, Begging-Lustre,
3 3/4", 2 holes

180 Duck-Japan, 5 1/2", 1 hole

181 Duckling(Chalk)-
4 3/4", 2 holes

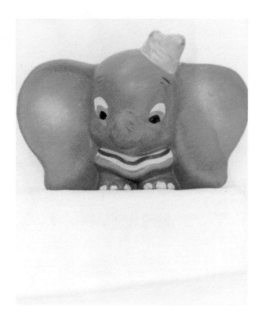

182 Dumbo(C)W.D.P.,
3", 3 holes

183 Elephant-Lustre, 3 1/2",
1 hole   (M)

184 Dutch Girl-Celluloid,
6 1/4", 1 hole

185 Ghost(6970),
8", 1 hole

186 Man w/Derby-Japan,
5 1/2", 2 holes

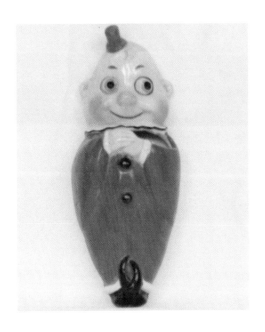

187 Palmer Cox Brownie -
Germany(6971), 5 1/2", 1 hole

188 Rabbit(Norwood)(T724)-
Germany, 5 1/2", 1 hole

189 Skeezix-(C)K-USA, Metal,
6", 2 holes

190- 195 Reserved

196 Aviator-Celluloid,
6 1/8", 1 hole

197 Girl-Celluloid, 4 7/8", 1 hole
198 Boy-Celluloid, 5", 1 hole

199 Cowboy-Japan, 4 1/2", 1 hole

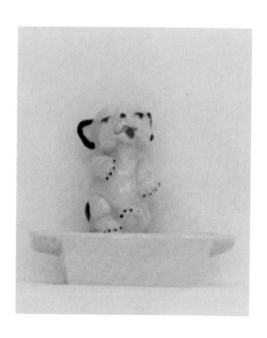

200 Dog, Begging-Germany(5442)
DER, 3", 1 hole

201 Dog w/Basket on Back-Japan
     (Goldcastle), 6", 2 holes

202 Dalmatian-Germany(105),
     4", 1 hole

203 Dutch Boy w/Cap - Japan, 5 1/4", 2 holes
204 Dutch Girl-Japan, 4 3/4", 2 holes (W)

205 Dutch Boy & Girl Sitting on
     Mantle-Japan(Goldcastle),
     4 1/4", 3 holes

206 Doctor w/Satchel-Japan,
5 3/4", 1 hole

207 Dutch Girl w/Large Hat,
5 1/2", 1 hole

208 Flower Child-base embossed
w/ "Snails" on 3 sides-
5 1/2", 2 holes

209 Frog w/Mandolin-Japan
(Goldcastle), 6", 1 hole

210 Little Red Riding Hood -
      Germany(DRGM), 5 1/2", 1 hole

211 Muggsy-Germany, 3 3/4", Holds
      brush in paw   (M)

212 Santa w/Sack & Lantern,
      5", 1 hole

213 Three Little Pigs-Japan
      (Goldcastle), 4", 3 holes (S)

214- 220 Reserved

221 Andy Gump & Min(Bisque) -
Japan, 4", 1 hole

222 Bell Hop w/Boots-Japan,
Arms hold brushes, 4 3/4"

223 Boy in Knickers-Japan,
4 3/4", 2 holes

224 Cat, Halloween, 4", 1 hole

225 Cat on Pedestal-Japan
(Diamond T), 5 7/8", 2 holes

226 Crow on Pedestal-Japan
(Diamond T), 6", 2 holes

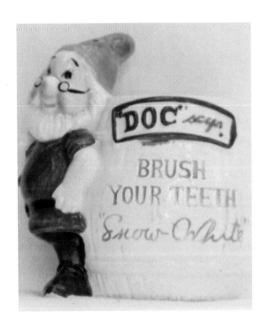

227 Doc(C)W.D.P., 4 1/4", 1 hole
"Brush Your Teeth, Snow White"

228 Dwarf "Happy"(C)WD(Bisque) -
Japan, 3 1/2", 1 hole   (M)

229 Fairy, Celluloid-Japan,
    4 3/4", 2 holes

230 Flapper-4 1/4", 2 holes

231 Mandolin Player,
    4 1/8", 1 hole

232 Mickey Mouse(C)W.E.D.(103) (Bisque)
Jointed Arm - Japan, 5", Arm holds brush (M)
233 Minnie Mouse(C)W.E.D.(104) (Bisque)
Jointed Arm - Japan, 5", Arm holds brush (M)

234 Mickey & Minnie (C)W.E.D. w/
     Hands on Hips(Bisque) - Japan,
     4 1/4", 2 holes

235 Mickey & Minnie Mouse
     w/Pluto (Bisque) (C)W.E.D.(S335) -
     Japan, 4 1/2", 2 holes

241 Orphan Annie & Sandy
     (C)FAS(S565)(Bisque) - Japan, 4" 2 holes

242 Pinocchio & Figaro(Shafford),
     5 1/4", 1 hole (M)

236-240 Reserved

243 Traffic Cop-Germany, "Don't
     Forget the Teeth", 5 1/4", 1 hole

244 Popeye(Bisque)-Japan,
     5", 1 hole   (M)

245 Skippy w/Jointed Arm(Bisque),
     5 5/8", Arm holds brush

246 Snow White(Geniune(C)W.D.)
     copyright foreign, 6", 1 hole (M)

247 Siamese Donald Duck (C)W.D. (S1102) -
Japan, 4 1/4", 2 holes   (M)

248 Three Bears w/Bowls-Japan
(KIM USUI), 4", 3 holes

249 The Lone Ranger(C)T.L.R.
(Chalk), 4", 1 hole

250 The Three Little Pigs w/Piano(C)W.D.
(Bisque), 5", 2 holes

251-260 Reserved

261 Betty Boop-(C)1983KFS,
     4 3/4", 4 holes

262 Bear w/Feet in Air-Germany,
     3 1/2", 2 holes

263 Big Bird(C) - M(Taiwan RCC),
     4 1/2", 2 holes

264 Bulldog-Japan, 3 1/2", 1 hole

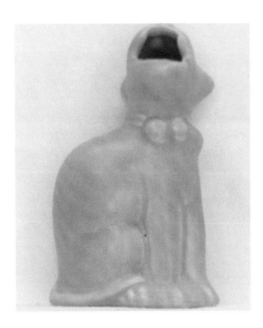

265 Cat - Howling(Red Wing 878),
    5", 1 hole

266 Duck-billed Platypus -
    Japan(TA), 4 1/4", 2 holes

267 Orphan Annie & Sandy on Couch-
    (Bisque)(C)FAS-Japan,
    3 3/4", 2 holes   (M)

268 Swami-Japan, 4", 1 hole

47

269-279 Reserved

280 Dog, Calico-Japan,
3 1/2"

281 Dog w/Sad Face-Germany(100),
3 3/4"

282 Elephant (Lustre)-Japan, 3"

283 Schnauzer-Germany 3 1/8", 2 holes

INDEX

INDEX

PRICE GUIDE

Plate No.	Price	Plate No.	Price
1. Baby Bunting	350-375	83. Donald Duck (Bisque)	250-275
2. Little Red Riding Hood	350-375	84. Ducky Dandy	150-175
3. Old Mother Hubbard	350-375	85. Dutch Girl w/Big Feet	80-90
4. Peter Rabbit	350-375	86. Dutch Girl w/Flowers	75-85
5-10 Reserved		87. Dutch Boy w/Hand on Hips	65-75
11. Annie Oakley	90-100	88. Dutch Boy & Girl Kissing	55-65
12. Baby Deer	85-95	89-92 Reserved	
13. Bear w/Jacket	80-90	93. Dwarfs in Front of Fence	1250-1275
13A. Bear w/Jacket	80-90	94. Elephant w/Trunk in Air	75-85
14. Bear	85-95	95. Elephant w/ Tusk	70-80
15. Bear, Gaytone	60-70	96. Genie	100-110
16. Bear w/Scarf & Hat	70-80	97. Giraffe	115-125
17-20 Reserved		98. Girl w/Doll	85-95
21. Bell Hop w/Flowers	65-75	99. Girl w/Dog & Bonnet	85-95
21A. Bell Hop w/Flowers	65-75	100. Girl w/Hat	80-90
22. Bonzo	80-90	101. Girl Powdering Nose	80-90
23. Bonzo w/ Side Tray, Lustre	125-135	102. Girl w/Basket	75-85
24. Boy Brushing Teeth	80-90	103. Girl Combing Boy's Hair	75-85
25. Boy w/Cap & Tie	65-75	104. Girl Washing Boy's Face	70-80
26. Boy w/Dog	70-80	105. Halloween Policeman	90-100
27. Girl w/Dog	70-80	106-110 Reserved	
28. Boy on Elephant	75-85	111. Harold Teen	1300-1350
29. Boy w/Top Hat	65-75	112. Henry & Henrietta	475-575
30. Boy w/Violin	70-80	113. Horse	70-80
31-35 Reserved		114. Humpty-Dumpty	100-125
36. Cat	70-80	115. Indian Chief	225-250
37. Cat, Calico	85-95	116. Kayo	100-125
38. Cat w/Bass Fiddle	110-120	117. Little Red Riding Hood	95-110
39. Chef	65-75	117A. Little Red Riding Hood	95-110
40. Children in Auto	70-80	118. Lion	75-85
41. Children, Big Brother	55-65	118A. Lion (Color Variant)	75-85
42. Children, Big Sister	55-65	119. Mary Poppins	125-135
43. Children, Boy w/Basket	60-65	120. Mexican Boy	80-90
44. Children, Girl w/Basket	60-65	121. Mickey, Donald & Minnie	325-350
45. Children, Girl w/Umbrella	65-75	122. Mickey & Pluto	250-300
46. Children, Boy w/Umbrella	65-75	123. Moon Mullins	90-100
47. Children, Little Sister	65-75	124. Muggsy (pair)	200-225
48. Children, Little Brother	65-75	125. Old King Cole	85-100
49-54 Reserved		126. Old Woman in Shoe	70-80
55. Circus Dog	75-85	127. Orphan Annie	100-130
56. Circus Elephant	75-85	128. Penguin	85-95
57. Clown, Large	65-75	129. Peter Pumpkin-Eater	75-85
58. Clown, Small	65-75	130. Peter Rabbit	90-120
59. Clown w/Bug on Nose	125-150	131. Pirate w/Large Boots	80-90
60. Clown, Juggling	75-85	132. Pirate w/Sash	80-90
61. Clown w/Mandolin	80-90	133. Pluto	300-325
62. Clown w/Mask	100-125	134. Pup, Begging	85-95
63-68 Reserved		135. Pup, "Brush for Health"	85-95
69. Cow	80-90	136. Pup w/Large Eyes	80-90
70. Cowboy Next to Cactus	75-85	137. Rabbit	80-90
71. Dachsund	70-80	138. Rabbit w/Containers	65-75
72. Dog w/Basket	80-90	139-144 Reserved	
73. Dog, Head Cocked	80-90	145. Sailors on Anchor	60-70
74. Dog, Smiling	65-75	146. Scottie Dogs	80-90
74A. Dog, Smiling (Variant)	65-75	147. "Siesta"	80-90
75. Dog w/Pup & Basket	70-80	148. Soldier	70-80
76-80 Reserved		149. Soldier w/Sash	70-80
81. Donkey	85-100	150. The Baker	70-80
82. Donkey w/Mane	85-100	151. The Butcher	70-80

Plate No.	Price	Plate No.	Price
152. The Candlestick Maker	70-80	221. Andy Gump & Min	70-80
153. The Three Bears	75-85	222. Bell Hop w/Boots	60-70
154. Tom, Tom, the Piper's Son	90-100	223. Boy in Knickers	65-75
155. Toonerville Trolley	500-550	224. Cat, Halloween	130-140
156. Uncle Walt	75-85	225. Cat on Pedestal	125-150
157. Uncle Willie	80-85	226. Crow on Pedestal	125-150
158-165 Reserved		227. "Doc"	85-95
166. Bird	70-80	228. Dwarf, "Happy"	600-625
167. Bear (Norwood)	85-95	229. Fairy (Celluloid)	90-100
168. Bear (Chalk)	45-55	230. Flapper	110-120
169. Bell Hop	60-70	231. Mandolin Player	90-100
170. Bonzo w/Tail	80-90	232. Mickey Mouse	400-425
171. Bonzo	70-80	233. Minnie Mouse	400-425
172. Carousel	100-110	234. Mickey & Minnie	275-300
173. Cat, Standing on Paws	90-100	235. Mickey, Minnie, & Pluto	275-300
174. Clown, Terra Cotta	70-80	236-240 Reserved	
175. Clown, Iron	200-225	241. Orphan Annie & Sandy	90-100
176. Clown w/Fancy Vest	75-85	242. Pinocchio & Figaro	450-475
177. Clown w/Ruffled Collar	75-85	243. Traffic Cop	325-350
178. Dog, "The Kirede"	85-95	244. Popeye	475-500
179. Dog, Begging (Lustre)	90-100	245. Skippy	90-100
180. Duck	80-90	246. Snow White	225-250
181. Duckling (Chalk)	35-45	247. Siamese Donald Duck	400-425
182. Dumbo	300-350	248. Three Bears w/Bowls	85-95
183. Elephant, Lustre	100-125	249. The Lone Ranger	70-80
184. Dutch Girl (Celluloid)	95-105	250. The Three Pigs	200-225
185. Ghost	75-85	251-260 Reserved	
186. Man w/Derby	75-85	261. Betty Boop	75-85
187. Palmer Cox Brownie	135-145	262. Bear w/Feet in Air	80-90
188. Rabbit (Norwood)	80-90	263. Big Bird	70-80
189. Skeezix, Metal	150-175	264. Bulldog	50-60
190-195 Reserved		265. Cat	85-95
196. Aviator (Celluloid)	110-120	266. Duck-Billed Platypus	80-90
197. Girl (Celluloid)	90-100	267. Orphan Annie & Sandy on Couch	110-135
198. Boy(Celluloid)	90-100	268. Swami	75-85
199. Cowboy	75-85	269-279 Reserved	
200. Dog, Begging	120-130	280. Calico Dog	55-65
201. Dog w/Basket on Back	90-100	281. Dog w/Sad Face	85-95
202. Dalmatian	150-175	282. Elephant, Lustre	85-95
203. Dutch Boy w/Cap	65-75	283. Schnauzer	90-100
204. Dutch Girl	65-75		
205. Dutch Boy & Girl on Mantle	95-105		
206. Doctor w/Satchel	90-100		
207. Dutch Girl w/Large Hat	90-100		
208. Flower Child	45-55		
209. Frog w/Mandolin	85-95		
210. Little Red Riding Hood	200-225		
211. Muggsy	250-275		
212. Santa w/Sack & Lantern	275-300		
213. Three Little Pigs	90-110		
214-220 Reserved			